Peace
of Heart

Additional titles in the *Thirty Days with a Great Spiritual Teacher* series

ALL WILL BE WELL
Based on the Classic Spirituality of *Julian of Norwich*

GOD AWAITS YOU
Based on the Classic Spirituality of *Meister Eckhart*

LET NOTHING DISTURB YOU
A Journey to the Center of the Soul with *Teresa of Avila*

SIMPLY SURRENDER
Based on the *Little Way of Térèse of Lisieux*

TRUE SERENITY
Based on Thomas A Kempis' *The Imitation of Christ*

YOU SHALL NOT WANT
A Spiritual Journey Based on *The Psalms*

WHERE ONLY LOVE CAN GO
A Journey of the Soul into *The Cloud of Unknowing*

Future titles in the series will focus on authors and classic works such as Hildegaard of Bingen, John of the Cross, Augustine, Catherine of Sienna, Brother Lawrence, and others.

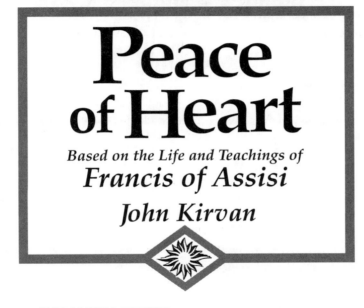

30 Days with a Great Spiritual Teacher

Peace of Heart

Based on the Life and Teachings of
Francis of Assisi

John Kirvan

AVE MARIA PRESS Notre Dame , Indiana 46556

John Kirvan is the editor and author of several books including *The Restless Believers*, and currently lives in southern California where he writes primarily about classic spirituality.

First printing, July, 1995
Third printing, April, 1999
35,000 copies in print

The morning meditation passages have been freely adapted from Thomas Celano's two *Lives of St Francis*. We wish to acknowledge our indebtedness to the translation by Placid Hermann, O.F.M., included in *St. Francis of Assisi, Omnibus of Sources*, © 1973, Franciscan Herald Press, Quincy, Illinois.

International Standard Book Number: 0-87793-564-5

Library of Congress Card Number: 95-77235

Cover and text design by Elizabeth J. French

Printed and bound in the United States of America

Contents

In all his preaching,
before he set forth the word of God
to those gathered about
Francis first prayed that they might have peace.
"The Lord give you peace," he would greet them.
For this reason many who had hated peace,
with the help of the Lord
embraced peace, with all their heart
and were made children of peace.

—Thomas of Celano, c. 1229

Francis of Assisi

Perhaps no one in Christian history has so caught the spiritual imagination of the Western world as has Brother Francis of Assisi. Certainly no one has broken through denominational and cultural boundaries in the way and to the extent he has.

The world has become unusually and universally comfortable with this extraordinary figure who has over the centuries come to be called: "the little poor man."

His image adorns gardens and parks everywhere, a tall, serene, undemanding figure who stands, hands outstretched to the birds of the air who come to rest on his shoulders, forest creatures at his feet, summoning up hope for a kinder, gentler world.

Francis did indeed preach to the birds, take pity on worms, walk gently over stones and acknowledge his brotherhood to the sun, the moon, and the stars.

But it is imperative, if we are to hear what he has to say to our spirit, to know at what price, with what commitment, with what spiritual daring he achieved the serenity that so attracts us.

Francis was no soft, fuzzy figure moving romantically through a gentle, even sentimental landscape, but a tough, hard, demanding revolutionary voyager of the spirit. Francis is not a messenger of cheap grace, salvation through warm feelings, a feel-good storyteller, a pacifier for the modern soul.

He was someone who chose to live not with easy metaphors of poverty, but in real, harsh, grinding "poorness."

Brother Fire was not the romantic warm glow of a hearth, but the searing pain of cauterized eyes. He loved all the world's creatures not because they were cute and cuddly—many are not—but because he saw in all of them a mirror of our common Creator.

This was a practical man who in effect founded and governed a worldwide, multilevel spiritual family which he conceived, directed, recruited for, and managed. He turned back the faint of heart and sent packing those who cheated on the literalness of the poverty which he expected of himself and of all who would be his spiritual companions.

Francis was born about 1181 into an affluent family and for his first twenty-five years developed a reputation for his self-indulgence and playfulness that made him a hero and leader of his town's young people. He was also a dreamer of adventurous dreams that led him into a war between cities where he was taken prisoner. He returned to Assisi unwillingly to take up where he had left off. He turned his back on a family business career and a return to the military heroics of his young dreams.

Three things, his biographers report, triggered his extraordinary life change. At the price of alienating his father and his long time companions he chose to rebuild a poor and abandoned church and to live in poverty as he did so. Then came a meeting with lepers. He overcame his long-held, deep repugnance to embrace these most abandoned of society. And at a Sunday mass, Christ's gospel appeal to sell all and come follow him, became an invitation to which he responded with a lifetime commitment.

You will find in these pages an almost relentless emphasis on real poverty and its necessary companion humility. This is so not just because these virtues are the key to Franciscan spirituality, but because in the view of Francis—and the gospels—they are the key to Christianity, the rock bottom message of Jesus.

What you will not find is a systematic theory of spirituality, and a step-by-step program for its realization. Francis was not a theologian, not a scholar, not a writer. He was an occasional poet and maker of prayers. He was the father of a spiritual family for whom he dictated rules and admonitions. But most basically he was someone who lived his vision. His life rather than his words teach us what it is like to meet God as Francis met and served him.

The morning readings in this book are developed from two *Lives of Francis* written by Thomas Celano in the years soon after the saint's death. Here we see Francis in action. Here we see his spirituality fleshed out in the world he wished to flee, but which he never rejected.

Here in "stories" we meet this extraordinary man whose response to the world of the thirteenth century gives shape and motivation to our response to the world of the twentieth. He chose to live as a poor man, envious only of those who had less than he. His poverty was as harsh, as painful as that of any modern urban street. His begging is as timely as the homelessness in our own streets and as insistent in its demands on our conscience.

The evening prayer uses a form beloved of Francis, a meditation on the words of the Lord's Prayer and on favorite passages of scripture. Each day ends with a variation on a passage from the book of Numbers (6:24-26), often called the "Priestly Prayer," that Francis once used as a personal blessing to his close companion, Leo.

This spiritual journey with Francis is marked not only by poverty and humility, but by the compassion that today is being rightfully restored to its place at the heart of any viable spirituality. Franciscan spirituality may in fact be the archetypal spirituality of our times. He knew and freely chose a poverty that is politically demanding and as institutionally challenging. Francis lived a spirituality of compassion rooted in poverty and humility.

It is, perhaps, the most exquisite of ironies, that this austere, spiritually-demanding figure rescued from garden tranquillity may be the most perfect guide for our times, and his spirituality the archetype for a hungry, avidly-searching generation.

How to Pray This Book

The purpose of this book is to open a gate for you, to make accessible the spiritual experience and wisdom of one of history's most important and most beloved spiritual teachers, Francis of Assisi.

This is not a book for mere reading. It invites you to meditate and pray its words on a daily basis over a period of thirty days.

It is a handbook for a spiritual journey.

Before you read the "rules" for taking this spiritual journey, remember that this book is meant to free your spirit not confine it. If on any day the meditation does not resonate well for you, turn elsewhere to find a passage which seems to best fit the spirit of your day and your soul. Don't hesitate to repeat a day as often as you like until you feel that you have discovered what the Spirit, through the words of the author, has to say to your spirit.

Here are suggestions on one way to use this book as a cornerstone of your prayers.

As Your Day Begins

As the day begins set aside a quiet moment in a quiet place to read the meditation suggested for the day

The passage is short. It never runs more than a couple of hundred words, but it has been carefully selected to give a spiritual focus, a spiritual center to your whole day. It is designed to remind you as another day begins of your own existence at a spiritual level. It is meant to put you in the presence of the spiritual master who is your companion and teacher on this journey. But most of all the purpose of the passage is to remind you that at this moment and at every moment during this day you will be living and acting in the presence of a God who invites you continually, but quietly to live in and through him.

A word of advice: read slowly. Very slowly. The meditation has been broken down into sense lines to help you do just this. Don't read to get to the end, but to savor each part of the meditation. You never know what short phrase, what word will trigger a response in your spirit. Give the words a chance. After all you are not just reading this passage, you are praying it. You are establishing a mood of serenity for your whole day. What's the rush?

All Through Your Day

Immediately following the day's reading you will find a single sentence which we call a mantra, a word borrowed from the Hindu tradition. This phrase is meant as a companion for your spirit as it moves through a busy day. Write it down on a 3" x 5" card or on the appropriate page of your daybook. Look at it as often as you can. Repeat it quietly to yourself and go on your way.

It is not meant to stop you in your tracks or to distract you from responsibilities but simply, gently, to remind you of the presence of God and your desire to respond to this presence.

As Your Day Is Ending

This is a time for letting go of the day.

Find a quiet place and quiet your spirit. Breathe deeply. Inhale, exhale—slowly and deliberately again and again until you feel your body let go of its tension.

Now read the evening prayer slowly, phrase by phrase. You may recognize at once that we have taken one of the most familiar evening prayers of the Christian tradition and woven into it phrases taken from the meditation with which you began your day and the mantra that has accompanied you all through your day. In this way, a simple evening prayer gathers together the spiritual character of the day that is now ending as it began—in the presence of God.

It is a time for summary and closure.

Invite God to embrace you with love and to protect you through the night.

Sleep well.

Some Other Ways to Use This Book

1. Use it anyway your spirit suggests. As mentioned earlier, skip a passage that doesn't resonate for you on a given day, or repeat for a second day or even several days a passage whose richness

speaks to you. The truths of a spiritual life are not absorbed in a day, or for that matter, in a lifetime. So take your time. Be patient with the Lord. Be patient with yourself.

2. Take two passages and/or their mantras—the more contrasting the better—and "bang" them together. Spend time discovering how their similarities or differences illumine your path.

3. Start a spiritual journal to record and deepen your experience of this thirty-day journey. Using either the mantra or another phrase from the reading that appeals to you, write a spiritual account of your day, a spiritual reflection. Create your own meditation.

4. Join the millions who are seeking to deepen their spiritual life by joining with others to form small groups. More and more

PEACE OF HEART

people are doing just this to aid and support each other in their mutual quest. Meet once a week, or at least every other week to discuss and pray about one of the meditations. There are lots of books and guides available to help you make such a group effective.

Thirty Days with
Francis of Assisi

Day One

◆◆◆◆◆

My Day Begins

There came a moment
when the Holy Spirit overtook
the young Francis.
The time had come for him
to follow the impulses of his soul.
He would turn to things of the spirit,
putting aside the worldly concerns
that had dominated his life.
He sold everything he had,

even the horse he was riding.
When he was still wondering
what to do with the money he had received from the sales
he came upon the old, crumbling church of St. Damian
and its poor old pastor.
At the old man's knees
he poured out his newly found spiritual hunger.
The old man was skeptical of such a sudden conversion
in a young man so well known till now
as the neighborhood's ring leader in riotous living.
He refused the money.
But Francis remained obstinate,
begging the old man to believe in his sincerity,
asking the priest over and over again
that for the sake of the Lord
he be allowed to stay at the church with him.

Finally the priest gave in.
Francis could stay
but out of fear of the young man's father,
the priest would not accept the money.

Francis then took the money
for which he no longer had use or desire
and threw it upon a windowsill to join the dust
that was gathered there.
For Francis,
the money was of no more importance than the dust.
Henceforth he would desire to possess only
that wisdom that is better than gold,
and to acquire that prudence
that is more precious than silver.
(1 Cel IV)

All Through the Day

Choose wisdom rather than gold.

(Prov 16:16)

My Day Is Ending

Our Father who art in heaven,
all through this day
I have meditated on what it might mean
to follow my deepest spiritual impulse,
to set aside worldly values
and surrender my life to your Holy Spirit.
Engender in me the wisdom
that is greater than gold,
the prudence that is more precious than silver.
Take me at my word.
And now as the day ends
and sleep approaches
I pray with Francis

that I will have the strength to choose
what the world values least.

May the Lord bless and keep all his children.
May he make his face to shine upon us
and be gracious to us.
May the Lord look kindly upon us,
grant us a quiet night and lasting peace.

Day Two

◆◆◆◆◆

My Day Begins

In the first days of his service to the Lord,
working to restore the church required that
he exchange a delicate privileged life
for that of a common laborer.
The strain was very noticeable to the old pastor
whose church he was repairing.
The hard work, the long days
were leaving Francis worn out.

The pastor, feeling sorry for him,
began each day to set out some special food,
not delicate because he was poor, but special.
The quiet kindness of the old man
was not lost on Francis.
He was deeply grateful,
but it also caused him concern.
"There will not be," he told himself,
"a thoughtful priest everywhere
to provide these special things.
This is not a life of true poverty.
Do not get used to it.
If you do, gradually you will return to the life
you have chosen to leave behind.
And again you will chase after its comforts.

Leave the table.
Go into the village and beg from door to door
and accept whatever they will give you."
And he did as his spirit commanded.

He collected a mixture of scraps almost too horrible to eat.
But he reminded himself
that he was the servant of the Lord
and that he must conquer himself.
He ate what he had collected.
He did it with joy of spirit reminding himself
that love makes the hard soft, the bitter sweet.
The way of Francis from the very beginning was
the way of the poor,
the way of common experience
the way of the common man.

(2 Cel 1, IX)

All Through the Day

You cannot live by bread alone.

(Lk 4:4)

My Day Is Ending

Our Father who art in heaven,
let me come to depend each day on that bread
which alone can nourish my spirit.
Let it sweeten that which is bitter,
make easier that which is hard.
Remind me always
that I have chosen to be your servant
and to accept your gifts whatever they be.
Nourish me at your table.
Take me at my word.
And now as the day ends
and sleep approaches
I pray with Francis

that you will give me the strength to leave behind
the comforts that the world offers.

May the Lord bless and keep all his children.
May he make his face to shine upon us
and be gracious to us.
May the Lord look kindly upon us,
grant us a quiet night and lasting peace.

Day Three

◆◆◆◆◆

My Day Begins

His father refused to honor the call
that Francis heard in his soul
and went in angry search of his son
determined to return him to his former life.
For a month Francis hid in a pit
dependent on others for food and every human need.
He prayed and wept and begged his Lord to deliver him.
In the past he had trusted his own efforts.
Now he cast his whole care upon the Lord.

And in the darkness of his prison
he began to experience an exquisite joy,
the like of which he had never before known.

He felt his soul catch fire
and he left his prison to face those
who were pursuing him.
His old friends refused to accept his new life
and greeted him with abuse.
They shouted at him that he was mad and demented.
They threw mud and stones.
He became the talk of the town.
But a patient man is stronger than a proud man.
Francis turned a deaf ear to their anger and hatred.
He remained unchanged and unbroken
by their anger and hatred.

He gave thanks to God.

It is useless to persecute someone
who is truly striving after virtue.
The more they are attacked
the more surely they will triumph.
To be humbled, it is said,
strengthens a generous spirit.

(1 Cel V)

All Through the Day

God is my helper,
he upholds my life.

(Ps 5:4)

My Day Is Ending

Our Father who art in heaven,
deliver me daily
from the world that I seek to leave behind.
If in the past I have depended on my own efforts,
teach me now to put my whole trust in you.
Be my helper,
the sole support of my life.
Free me from the prison of the world.
Let me turn a deaf ear to the call of its values
Lead me not into temptation.
Take me at my word.
And now as the day ends
and sleep approaches

I pray with Francis
that you will deliver me from darkness into joy
the like of which I have never known.

May the Lord bless and keep all his children.
May he make his face to shine upon us
and be gracious to us.
May the Lord look kindly upon us,
grant us a quiet night and lasting peace.

Day Four

◆◆◆◆◆

My Day Begins

Inevitably word reached his father
that Francis was the center and target
of commotion in the streets.
He immediately went in search of his son,
not to rescue him, but to destroy him.
He was like a wolf pursuing a sheep.
And when he found his son
he dragged him home in shame and disgrace.
Without mercy or compassion

he consigned his son to darkness for days on end,
determined to recover the worldly-wise child
he had known and understood.
At first he used words
Then came physical blows and finally chains.
But Francis, rather than being broken,
was instead strengthened
and made more certain of his new purpose in life.
Neither the insults of his father's words
nor the exhaustion of his being chained
cut into his patience.

For he who has learned from the Lord
to find his joy in tribulation
is not easily diverted from his determination
or separated from the flock of Christ.

Scourging and chains are not enough.
He is not drowned by a flood of hatred and opposition,
but finds a safe harbor
in the Son of God,
who when our troubles seem too hard,
even overwhelming to us,
reminds us that his were even greater.

(1 Cel V)

All Through the Day

You are my safety.

(Ps 32:7)

My Day Is Ending

Our Father who art in heaven,
grant me a safe haven.
Deliver me from all evil,
and let every misunderstanding of what I seek,
every obstacle,
serve only to strengthen my desire
to live in you and in you alone.
Let me not grow weary,
but remind me
when trouble threatens to overwhelm me,
how much greater were your Son's.
And now as the day ends

and sleep approaches
I pray with Francis
that you will make me more certain of my new purpose.

May the Lord bless and keep all his children.
May he make his face to shine upon us
and be gracious to us.
May the Lord look kindly upon us,
grant us a quiet night and lasting peace.

Day Five

My Day Begins

Even before he fell under the spell of God's grace,
Francis practiced what he would one day preach.
While he was still very much of the world
he found the sight of lepers so loathsome
that he would come no closer to their homes
than two miles
and even then he would hold his nose.
But one day, he met a leper,
and moved suddenly by grace, he kissed the man.

From that day on he began more and more
to feel shame and distaste at his behavior
until by the mercy of the Redeemer
he overcame his repugnance.

And while still of the world
he would often naturally and spontaneously
stretch forth his hand to those who had nothing,
and show compassion to the afflicted.
One day contrary to his custom
for he was by nature courteous,
he turned away from a certain poor man
who had asked for alms in the name of God.
He was instantly sorry.
He told himself it was a great shame and reproach
to withhold alms that were asked of him

in the name of so great a king.
He therefore resolved in his heart never in the future
to refuse anyone if at all possible,
who asked for the love of God.
This he most diligently carried out
long before he sacrificed himself entirely
and in every way.
He became a practitioner of the evangelical counsels
long before he preached them.
"Give to him who begs from you," he said;
"and do not refuse him who would borrow from you."
(1 Cel VII)

All Through the Day

Give to those who beg of you,
do not refuse those who are in need.

(Mt 5:42)

My Day Is Ending

Our Father who art in heaven,
let me never forget
that you do not always come to us wrapped in beauty
your face easily recognized.
You will be present in what repels us,
in what is inconvenient and annoying.
Let me see your face and hear your voice
in everyone I meet.
In your mercy
replace my repugnance with your compassion.
Let me embrace those from whom I wish to turn away.
And now as the day ends
and sleep approaches

I pray with Francis
that I will recognize you in every face.

May the Lord bless and keep all his children.
May he make his face to shine upon us
and be gracious to us.
May the Lord look kindly upon us,
grant us a quiet night and lasting peace.

Day Six

❖❖❖❖❖

My Day Begins

One day during mass the gospel
spoke to Francis in a special way.
Disciples of Christ, he heard the gospel say,
should not possess gold or silver or money.
As they go on their way
they should not carry scrip
or wallet or bread or staff.
They should not have shoes
or two tunics.

They should preach the kingdom of God
and penance.

His response was immediate and joyful
"This is meant for me.
This is what I have longed to hear.
This is how with all my heart I wish to live."
He began immediately
to live out the word of the gospel.
He took off his shoes,
abandoned his staff,
kept only one tunic,
and replaced his leather belt with one small cord.
To keep the world's temptations at a distance
he designed for himself a simple tunic
that resembled a cross.

He made it of especially rough material
that he might do penance.
He made it so simple and meager
that no one could be envious.

All that he had heard in the reading of the gospel
he hurried to make part of his life.

Francis was not a passive listener to the gospel.
He took seriously what it was saying.
He committed it to memory.
He tried with great diligence to carry it out literally.
(1 Cel IX)

All Through the Day

If you would be perfect,
go, sell what you possess,
give to the poor . . .
and come follow me.

(Mt 19:21)

My Day Is Ending

Our Father who art in heaven,
it is easy to let the words of the gospel wash over me,
almost unheard and unheeded,
their demands softened
and left for others.
Let me understand that they are meant for me.
They are what I need to hear.
This is how you wish me to live.
At whatever cost
let me make part of my life
all that I hear in your gospel.
Let me not be a passive listener, but a doer of your word.

And now as the day ends and sleep approaches
I pray with Francis
to hear your words as you mean them to be heard.

May the Lord bless and keep all his children.
May he make his face to shine upon us
and be gracious to us.
May the Lord look kindly upon us,
grant us a quiet night and lasting peace.

Day Seven

◆◆◆◆◆

My Day Begins

What others considered to be wealth,
Francis considered to be a trifle.
His ambitions were higher.
He longed to be poor with all his heart.
The world might flee and abhor poverty
but he knew that is was treasured
by the Son of God.
Poverty became his spouse, the love of his life.
He loved her beauty,

he abandoned his father and his mother
that he might hold her more closely.
He surrendered everything else that they might be as one.
Not for even an hour was he unfaithful to her.
This, he told his followers, was the way to perfection,
the guarantee of eternal riches.
No one desired gold as he desired poverty,
no one guarded their riches
as he guarded this jewel of the gospel.
Nothing upset him more
than to see in his companions anything
that was contrary to poverty.
From the beginning of his religious life until he died,
his riches consisted of only a tunic, cord, drawers
and nothing else.

The poverty of his habit proclaimed where his riches were.

In this way he went through life
happy, secure, and confident.
He traded the treasures of this world
for a hundred-fold reward.

(2 Cel 2, XXV)

All Through the Day

Everyone who leaves their home
or their brothers and sisters,
their father or mother, or their children and lands
for my sake,
will be rewarded a hundred times over
and know eternal life.

(Mt 19:29)

My Day Is Ending

Our Father who art in heaven,
teach me how
to leave behind the treasures of this world
for the hundred-fold reward of your kingdom.
Let me understand as Francis understood
that the wealth of this world is just a trifle in your eyes,
that what the world fears and abhors
can be the love of one's life,
a spouse of great beauty, a faithful companion.
Grant me the courage to seek those riches that last.
And now as the day ends and sleep approaches
I pray with Francis
that I might enjoy as he did,

the security, the comfort, and the confidence
that is the reward of poverty
embraced in your name and for your sake.

May the Lord bless and keep all his children.
May he make his face to shine upon us
and be gracious to us.
May the Lord look kindly upon us,
grant us a quiet night and lasting peace.

Day Eight

◆◆◆◆◆

My Day Begins

Once, late in the day,
tired and hungry after a long journey,
Francis and his companions came to a desert place.
But it was so far from any dwellings
they could find no food.
Suddenly a man appeared with some bread
and then immediately disappeared.
Their wonderment grew into a determination
to place even greater trust in divine providence.

For the next fifteen days
they moved to another isolated place
where they were visited by almost no one,
leaving their desert only to beg for food in a nearby town.
They ate what little they gathered
with great gratitude and deeply joyful hearts.

They rejoiced not only in their poverty
but in their isolation.
They determined to adopt everywhere the poverty
which in this place was giving them
so much spiritual consolation.
But they left the place nonetheless
for fear that if they were to stay too long
a sense of ownership might overtake their joy in poverty.
After this experience,
they all conferred with Francis

about whether they should dwell in the midst of people
or live in the solitude they had come to love.
Francis, who never trusted his own wisdom,
prayed long before making his choice.
He would not live for himself alone
but for him who died for all.

(1 Cel XIV)

All Through the Day

He died for everyone, that those who live
might no longer live just for themselves.

(2 Cor 5:15)

My Day Is Ending

Our Father who art in heaven,
let your kingdom come into my heart
not for my sake,
but for the sake of all those
for whom your Son lived and died.
Lead me not into the temptation
to take your great gifts and hoard them
in isolation and silence,
in selfish enjoyment of your presence.
Rather let me live so that others might have life.
And now as the day ends, Father,
and sleep approaches
open my heart to everyone,
give me the gift of a generous spirit.

For all your children I pray:
May the Lord bless and keep all of us.
May he make his face to shine upon us
and be gracious to us.
May the Lord look kindly upon us,
grant us a quiet night and lasting peace.

Day Nine

·◆·◆·◆·◆·

My Day Begins

To every town, to everyone,
Francis proclaimed the kingdom of God.
He preached peace, he taught salvation,
he demanded penance for the forgiveness of sins.
He did so not with great eloquence
and the strength of human reasoning,
but with the power of the Spirit.
He preached boldly,
flattering no one, offering no seductive promises.

He did not make light of sin,
but struck sharply at it wherever he found it.
He could do so because he did not rely on his words,
but on the example of his life.
He practiced before he preached.

From the poorest to the most learned
people flocked from everywhere to hear the holy man
and to embrace a new life.
His message seemed to them
like a light sent from heaven.
The face of the land changed.
Cheerfulness replaced the dour face of sin.
New growth sprang up in neglected fields.
Untended vines gave way to new blossoms that
proclaimed the Lord.
The land brought forth new fruit.

Thanksgiving and praise blossomed everywhere
and many put aside their worldly lives
to learn from the blessed preacher
how to love and revere their Creator.
To everyone
he presented new standards of living.
He demonstrated the way of salvation
in every walk of life.
(1 Cel XV)

All Through the Day

I have come that you might have life
and have it in abundance.

(Jn 10:10)

My Day Is Ending

Our Father who art in heaven,
renew with your love the face of our land.
Let new life spring up
where now there is only hopelessness and fear.
Let the forgotten of our world blossom
under your tender care.
Let your peace transform our warring hearts.
From the most neglected to the most privileged,
let your word be heard.
Grant especially that I may be an instrument
of your love and your peace.
And now as the day ends and sleep approaches
I pray with Francis

for the grace to embrace a new life,
that everywhere your joy may replace our sorrow.

May the Lord bless and keep all his children.
May he make his face to shine upon us
and be gracious to us.
May the Lord look kindly upon us,
grant us a quiet night and lasting peace.

Day Ten

◆◆◆◆◆

My Day Begins

One day Francis and his followers came to a valley
where birds of many kinds were gathered.
When he saw them
Francis left his companions and ran towards the birds.
They apparently were waiting for him.
Instead of taking wing as they would usually do
they stayed while he spoke to them.
"My companions, the birds," he said,
"you should praise your Creator very much

and always love him;
he gave you feathers to clothe you,
wings so that you might fly,
and everything else that you need.
God has made you most noble of his creatures,
giving you a home in the purity of the air;
and though you neither sow nor reap,
he protects and governs you
without any anxiety on your part."

The birds began to crane their necks,
extend their wings,
open their mouths, and gaze at him.
Then he blessed them,
and making the sign of the cross over them,
he gave them permission to fly away to some other place.

Then he went his own way
rejoicing and giving thanks to God
whom all creatures venerate humbly
and in their own way.

From that day on
he solicitously admonished all birds,
all animals and reptiles,
and even creatures that have no feeling
to praise and love their Creator.
Daily, when the name of the Savior had been invoked,
he saw and experienced their obedience.

(1 Cel XXI)

All Through the Day

Let the whole earth and its peoples
sing joyfully,
praising the Lord
with songs and shouts of joy.

(Ps 98:4)

My Day Is Ending

Our Father who art in heaven,
the whole earth is yours and all that inhabit it.
May we never forget in our pride
that we are not your only creations.
Never cease to remind us
that we are bound to love and care for all of your creation
even as you love and care for us.
Open our eyes and hearts to all that you have made.
Let us give voice to those who are speechless
and love and praise you in their name.
Now as the day ends

and sleep approaches
let us rejoice and give thanks
to our common Creator.

May the Lord bless and keep all his creatures.
May he make his face to shine upon us
and be gracious to us.
May the Lord look kindly upon us,
grant us a quiet night and lasting peace.

Day Eleven

◆◆◆◆◆

My Day Begins

As the apostle Paul had taught him,
Francis sought not what was for him alone,
but rather what in his eyes would be most helpful
for the salvation of others.
Above all else
he desired to be alone with Christ.
More than anything else
he desired to be free of this world
lest it deprive him of his serenity.

He closed off every sound that he could,
blocking his senses,
deafening himself to any prompting of nature
that would take him away
from being alone with God.
Therefore he frequently chose solitary places
so that he could direct his mind solely to God.
"In the clefts of the rock he would build his nest
and in the hollow places of the wall his dwelling."

(Cant 2:14)

Nonetheless he never neglected his neighbor.
When he saw the time was opportune,
he willingly took care of things
pertaining to their salvation.
Yet his safest haven was prayer,
not prayer of a single moment,

or idle or presumptuous prayer,
but prayer of long duration,
full of devotion,
serene in humility.

Walking, sitting, eating, or drinking
he was always intent on prayer.
He would even go alone at night to pray
in abandoned churches located in deserted places,
and there under the protection of divine grace
he overcame many fears
and many disturbances of mind.

(1 Cel XXVII)

All Through the Day

For me to live is Christ,
to die is gain.

(Phil 1:21)

My Day Is Ending

Our Father who art in heaven,
I desire with all my heart to be alone with you.
You know how deeply I yearn for that silence
where yours is the only voice that can be heard.
I need to shut out the voice of the world,
and even of those who call out to me in your name.
I yearn for a safe haven,
a place of serenity,
where for more than a stolen moment
I can bask joyfully, quietly in your presence.
And even when this is not possible
let me never, whether walking, sitting, working,
eating, or sleeping, depart from your presence.
Now especially as this day ends

and the quiet of sleep approaches,
wrap me in your silence
and hear the wordless prayers of my soul.

May you, O Lord, bless and keep us:
Make your face to shine upon us,
and be gracious to us.
Look kindly, Lord, upon us.
Grant us a quiet night, lasting peace,
and a share in your everlasting silence.

Day Twelve

◆◆◆◆◆

My Day Begins

Francis was the father of the poor.
On one occasion
a follower of Francis turned on a poor man
who had asked for money:
"How do I know that you are not a rich man
pretending to be poor?"
The response deeply saddened, even angered Francis
who rebuked the brother.

He commanded him to strip before the poor man,
kiss his feet and beg his pardon.
"Anyone," Francis would often say,
"who hurts the poor, hurts Christ.
The poor are an image of Christ
who made himself poor for us."

It was not unusual for him,
when he found a poor person loaded down with wood
or other burdens,
to offer to take the load upon himself,
even though his shoulders were very weak.
It upset him to find someone poorer than himself,
not out of some false sense of vanity,
but because of an unending sense of compassion.
Even though his own cloak was poor indeed

he longed to share it with anyone who had less.

He would ask the rich in cold weather
to give him a mantle or furs
on the condition that they never expected
to have it returned.
The fur would go to the next poor person he met.

This father of the poor
made himself like the poor in every way.
(1 Cel XXVIII)

All Through the Day

Blessed are you when you consider the poor.

(Ps. 41:1)

My Day Is Ending

Our Father who art in heaven,
you bless the poor and the weak
and those who make themselves so for their sake.
You protect them in times of trouble.
You preserve their lives.
They are the blessed of your kingdom.
You do not allow their enemies
to triumph over their weakness.
You help them when they are sick.
You restore them to health.
You upset the world's order.
You reverse all our values.
Now as the day ends and sleep approaches

consider the poverty of my soul
and deliver me from all evils.

Bless and keep all your children,
especially the poor.
Make your face to shine upon us
and be gracious to us.
Look kindly upon us,
grant us a quiet night and lasting peace.

PEACE OF HEART

Day Thirteen

My Day Begins

It is almost impossible to describe
how great was the affection of Francis
for all of God's creation,
the depth of his joy in contemplating
the wisdom, the power, and the goodness
of their Creator in all creatures.
It was with this joy that he looked upon the sun,
beheld the moon, and gazed upon the stars.
He saw their Creator even in little worms,

which he would pick up from the road
and put down in a safe place lest they be trampled,
for he remembered that it had been said of his Lord,
"I am a worm and no man."
In winter he provided the bees with honey
lest they freeze.

He had a special love of flowers.
He preached to them
and invited them to praise the Lord
as though they could understand.
He urged cornfields and vineyards, stones and forest,
and everything green,
gardens, fountains and fields,
earth, fire, wind, and water,
to love God and serve him willingly.

PEACE OF HEART

He invited all creation
to imitate the youths in the fiery furnace
and praise and glorify the Creator of the universe.

Filled with the Spirit of God,
he never ceased to glorify, praise, and bless
in all creation
the Creator and Ruler of all things.
He called all creatures brother,
and in an extraordinary way unknown to others,
his sensitive heart
uncovered the hidden things of the world.
It was as though he were already enjoying
the freedom of the glory
of the sons of God.

(1 Cel XXIX)

All Through the Day

All of creation shall be set free.

(Rom 8:21)

My Day Is Ending

Our Father, Lord of creation,
hallowed be your name
in all that you have made.
Fill us with your Spirit
that we might always and in all your creatures
glorify, praise, and bless you.
In the wondrous works of your hands,
in the sun, the moon, and the stars,
in the flowers of the fields,
in everything that grows,
you make present to us your wisdom,
your power, and your goodness.
Now as the day ends

and sleep approaches,
bless and keep all of creation.
Out of the silent darkness of our brother the night sky
make your face to shine upon us
and be gracious to us.
Look kindly upon us,
grant us a quiet night
and lasting peace.

Day Fourteen

◆◆◆◆◆

My Day Begins

Bernard, a young man, first came to Francis
with a question:
"If someone has for a long time been the recipient of gifts from
a generous Lord
but no longer wishes to keep these gifts,
what would be the perfect thing to do?"
"Give them back," Francis replied, "to the Lord from whom
you have received them."

"Everything I have," said Bernard,
"I have been given by God,
and I am ready at your advice
to give them back to him."

Early the next morning
together they went to the church
and after saying a prayer for guidance
they took the book of the gospels,
opening it at random,
prepared to follow what counsel it gave.

They opened the book and read:
"If you would be perfect,
go, sell what you possess, and give to the poor."
(Mt 19:21)

They opened the book a second time and read:
"take nothing for your journey."
(Lk 9:3)

And a third time:
"If any man would come after me,
let him deny himself."
(Lk 9:23)

Without delay
Bernard did all these things
and never went against the advice
he had found in the gospel,
not an iota of it.
(2 Cel 1, X)

All Through the Day

If you wish to come after me,
you must deny yourself.

My Day Is Ending

Our Father who art in heaven,
everything I have has come from you.
If I am to follow you as I desire
I must now give it all back
by letting go of everything
that has a hold on me:
everything on which I am dependent,
everything that gives me security.
I must become poor,
dependent only on you.
Now as the day ends
and sleep approaches
let me leave the world behind

and surrender myself and all I have to you,
only to you.

Hear my prayer:
Make your face to shine upon us
and be gracious to us.
Look kindly upon us,
grant us a quiet night
and lasting peace.

PEACE OF HEART

Day Fifteen

◆◆◆◆◆

My Day Begins

The life of Francis was marked by miracles,
by extraordinary insights into the lives
of his brothers and sisters, by prophecies,
and by many other unusual blessings and gifts.

Such blessings should not surprise us.
The soul of Francis was not darkened
by earthly concerns.
Pleasures of the flesh were under control.
His mind was free to take flight.

The Word gave light and life to his words.
While he lived
quiet and peace filled his days
and there was an abundance of good things.
Holiness shone forth among the companions.
His words were filled with power.
The things of this world were plentiful
because eternal things were treasured.

How different we are!
We are immersed in darkness
and do not recognize what alone is necessary.
We do not share in his extraordinary gifts
because we are still tied to the flesh,
still dusty with earth's concerns.
We need to lift up our hearts to heaven.

We need to choose eternal life.
Then we would recognize what we do not yet know,
namely God and ourselves.
Bound to earth we see only the earth.
Only if our eyes are fixed on heaven
will we be able to see the things of heaven.
(2 Cel XXIII-IV)

All Through the Day

To you, O Lord, I lift up my soul.
In you alone, my God, I place my trust.

(Ps. 25:1)

My Day Is Ending

Our Father who art in heaven,
let the eyes of my soul be fixed on you,
let my trust be placed in you.
Let your will for me be done,
on earth as it is in heaven.
I am still immersed in darkness,
still unable to accept what alone is necessary.
Let me come to see myself
as you see me.
Let me see you as you are.
Now as the day ends
and sleep approaches
to you I entrust my life.

With Francis who trusted you completely I pray:
Bless us and keep us.
Make your face to shine upon us
and be gracious to us.
Look kindly upon us,
grant us a quiet night
and lasting peace.

Day Sixteen

❖❖❖❖❖

My Day Begins

One day,
when Francis was thinking about
the tender mercies with which the Lord had blessed him,
he began to wish that the Lord might show him
what the future held for him and his companions.
He sought out a place of prayer
as he had so often done before,
and he remained there for a long time.

He stood before the Lord of the whole earth,
in fear and trembling.
And he thought in the depths of his troubled soul
of the years he had spent wretchedly,
frequently repeating this phrase:
"God be merciful to me, a sinner."

Little by little a certain unspeakable joy
and a great sweetness began to flood his innermost heart.
As his anxiety began to recede
and the darkness that had gathered in his heart
because of his sin disappeared,
there was poured into him
a certainty that all his sins had been forgiven
and a confidence that grace had been restored to him.

It was almost as though he had left his body
and become enveloped in an all encompassing light.
His mind opened wide and
the future was opened to him.

The moment passed.
But Francis came away from it,
his vision revived,
a new person.
(1 Cel XI)

All Through the Day

God show your mercy to me, a sinner.

(Lk 18:13)

My Day Is Ending

Our Father who art in heaven,
I am here before you
not because I am worthy of your presence,
but to confess that I am a sinner.
Be merciful to me and grant to me
that unspeakable joy, that great sweetness
that once flooded the soul of Francis.
Let my anxiety recede,
the darkness of my heart disappear,
knowing that you have forgiven all my sins.
Now as the day ends
and sleep approaches
be merciful to me and to all your children.

Bless us and keep us.
Make your face to shine upon us
and be gracious to us.
Look kindly upon us,
grant us a quiet night
and lasting peace.

PEACE OF HEART

Day Seventeen

◆◆◆◆◆

My Day Begins

When Francis returned from his time of prayer
and the consolation of those moments,
he called all his companions together
and spoke to them of what was to come.

"My brothers," he said,
"we must give thanks to the Lord our God
in true faith and devotion
for all the gifts he has already given us.

But we must also be prepared
for the days to come."

He told them many things
concerning the Kingdom of God,
"You must despise this world's values,
renounce your own will,
and subdue the demands of your body."

"Go therefore my companions
two by two into the world
and announce to everyone
peace and repentance
unto the forgiveness of sins."

"Be patient with what sufferings you endure
for you can be sure that the Lord

PEACE OF HEART

has a purpose for you
and he will keep his promises."

"Answer humbly those who question you."

"Thank those who injure or humiliate you."

"Be obedient to your calling
with great joy and gladness."

"An eternal kingdom awaits you."

"Cast your care upon the Lord
and he shall uphold you."
(1 Cel XII)

All Through the Day

To save your life
you must lose it:
but if you lose your life for my sake
you will save it.

(Mk 8:35)

My Day Is Ending

Our Father who art in heaven,
thy kingdom come,
thy will be done,
on earth as it is in heaven.
Prepare me for the days that are to come.
Help me to reach out to everyone within my world
and, at whatever cost,
extend to them
the peace and forgiveness
that you have lavished on me.
And now as the day ends
and sleep approaches
I give you thanks for all the gifts
that you have already given to me

and to all the children of your kingdom.

Lord bless and keep all of us.
Make your face to shine upon us
and be gracious to us.
Look kindly, Lord, upon us,
grant us a quiet night
and lasting peace.

Day Eighteen

❖❖❖❖❖

My Day Begins

There was a time
when a doctor visited Francis every day
to care for his eyes.
One day Francis turned to his companions and said:
"Invite the doctor to dinner
and feed him something very good."
"How can we," the brother said,
"we are ashamed to offer him what we have.
We have so little."

"Do as I have asked," Francis said.
And the doctor, overhearing the exchange, said:
"My dear companions
nothing could be more delicious to me
than to share your poverty."
The companions set the table with what they had.
There was a little bread. Some wine.
And the luxury of a few vegetables.
Just as they sat down there was a knock at the door
and answering they found a woman
who offered them a basket of fine bread,
fishes, lobster, pies, honey, and grapes.
They sat down to a fine meal.
The doctor and the companions alike recognized
that they had been present for a miracle
that testified to the holiness of their host.

Their heavenly father does not forget his children
for the poorer they are
the more they need his care.
The poor are invited
to a more abundant table than the tyrants,
for God is more generous than man.

(2 Cel 1 XV)

All Through the Day

Where are we to find enough bread in the desert
to feed so many people?

(Mt 15:33)

My Day Is Ending

Our Father who art in heaven,
nourish my spirit
with the daily bread
that only you can provide.
For too long I have tried to live
on what I could provide for myself,
scraps of empty knowledge long gone stale.
I am hungry.
Feed me.
The whole world is hungry,
only you have bread enough
to feed so great a crowd, so deep a need.
Now especially as this day ends

and sleep approaches,
hear my prayer and those of all your children.
Let us not go to sleep hungry.
Bless and keep all of us:
Make your face to shine upon us
and be gracious to us.
Look kindly, Lord, upon us,
grant us a quiet night and lasting peace.

Day Nineteen

◆◆◆◆◆

My Day Begins

It was Easter.
The companions set the table
far more gracefully than usual
with fine linens and glass.
When Francis came down from his cell
he saw the luxurious setting.
He was not pleased.
He retraced his steps,
borrowed a poor man's hat,

picked up his staff,
and went outside to wait for the meal to begin.
When his companions began to eat,
he cried to them from the doorway:
"For the love of God,
alms to this poor wanderer."
"You are welcome," they said,
"for the love of the God
in whose name you have come."
He immediately entered
and sat before them in the ashes.
"My companions," he said,
"I am sitting as you should sit.
More than any others
we should be moved by the example of poverty
that we have been given by the Son of God.

The table you decorated
is not the table of the poor
who must go from door to door begging."

In this Francis was imitating that other pilgrim
who was alone in Jerusalem on that day,
the pilgrim
who made the hearts of his disciples
burn within them
as he spoke to them.
(2 Cel 1 XXI)

All Through the Day

Did not our hearts burn within us when he talked with us on the road?

(Lk 24:32)

My Day Is Ending

Our Father who art in heaven,
accompany me along the way,
for you alone
can give true direction to my journey.
You alone can cut through the chorus of voices
that threatens to deafen my soul
with empty promises and false hopes.
Your words alone
can make my soul burn within me.
Speak to me.
And now as the day ends, Father,
and sleep approaches,
still the voices of a noisy world.

Accompany me into the dark
with the light of your promises.

For myself, I pray, and for all your children:
May the Lord bless and keep all of us.
May he make his face to shine upon us
and be gracious to us.
May the Lord look kindly upon us,
grant us a quiet night and lasting peace.

PEACE OF HEART

Day Twenty

◆◆◆◆◆

My Day Begins

Confronted with companions who sought comfort
Francis would say:
"When we lose our taste for the spirit
then the demands of flesh and blood take over.
If the soul is not satisfied,
then what remains but the needs of the body?
Our animal needs become necessities
and our body forms our conscience."
We must be careful of what we deem to be necessary.

"When we depart from poverty
the world will abandon us.
We will seek and not find.
But when we embrace Lady Poverty,
the world will embrace us
because in our poverty
we have been given to the world
for the sake of its salvation."

Francis was bound to Lady Poverty
by an unbroken commitment.
Her rewards, he knew and preached,
are not in the present moment
but in the future.
His favorite psalms, the ones he most loved to chant,
were those that spoke of poverty.

"The needy shall not always be forgotten
and the hope of the poor shall not perish forever."
(Ps 9:18)

"Let the oppressed see it and be glad."
(Ps 69:32)
(2 Cel 1, XXXIX, XL)

All Through the Day

Let the oppressed see it and take hope.

(Ps 68:33)

PEACE OF HEART

My Day Is Ending

Our Father who art in heaven,
if your will is to be done on earth,
I cannot fool myself about my responsibility
to the poor and the oppressed.
Their poverty is not a metaphor.
Their hunger is real.
Their homelessness is real.
My commitment to them must be as real.
I must not forget or ignore their pain.
Their hope must not be allowed to perish.
And now as the day ends, and sleep approaches
open my heart to those in need,
grant me the gift of practical compassion.

For all your children,
but especially for the poor and the homeless
I pray:

May the Lord bless and keep all of us.
May he make his face to shine upon us
and be gracious to us.
May the Lord look kindly upon us,
grant us a quiet night and lasting shelter.

Day Twenty-One

◆◆◆◆◆

My Day Begins

Often, when invited by the wealthy to share their table,
Francis would first go from door to door
begging for scraps of food.
Only then would he join his hosts.
Asked why he did this, he replied:
"My inheritance is the kingdom of God
which shall last forever.
I shall not surrender it for passing riches.

It is poverty that makes us heirs and kings,
not the riches of this world."

On one such occasion
when he was a guest of a bishop
he brought to the table the scraps that he had begged
and passed them among the other guests
much to the embarrassment of the bishop.
"My brother," the bishop said,
"why have you shamed me in my own house?"
"I have not shamed you," Francis said,
"but brought you honor
by honoring a greater Lord,
a Lord who is pleased with poverty that we choose.
Our dignity consists in following this Lord
who became poor for us.

I enjoy much more a table
that is set out with scraps that are begged
than from a table laden with delicacies."

And the bishop said:
"Do what seems good to you
for the Lord is with you."
(2 Cel 2, XLII-III)

All Through the Day

Though he was rich,
he became poor for your sake,
so that in and through his poverty
you might become rich.

(2 Cor 8:9)

My Day Is Ending

Our Father who art in heaven,
your kingdom is my inheritance,
let me not settle for less.
Let me remember
that the privileged of your kingdom
are not the rich of this world,
but the poor,
that honor in your kingdom
is in following your Son
who became poor for our sake.
Now as the day ends and sleep approaches,
open my heart to those in need,
count me among the privileged of your kingdom.

For all your children
but especially for the poor and the homeless pray:
Lord bless and keep all of us.
Make your face to shine upon us
and be gracious to us.
Look kindly, Lord, upon us,
grant us a quiet night
and lasting citizenship in your kingdom.

Day Twenty-Two

◆◆◆◆◆

My Day Begins

Who has the right words to describe
Francis' compassion for the poor?
He had, it is true, a natural kindness.
But grace doubled it.
His soul could not resist the poor
and even when he could not give them alms,
he showered them with his affection.
For when he saw someone in need,
he saw Christ.

When he came upon the nakedness of the poor,
he saw Mary's son naked in her arms.

One day a poor and sickly man
came to where Francis was preaching.
Touched by the man's double affliction,
his poverty and his illness,
Francis spoke to his companion:
"When you see a poor man, brother,
you should see in him Christ and his mother.
It is the same when you come across a sick person.
See in him Christ
and consider the infirmities
that Christ took upon himself for our sake."
He always looked upon the face of Christ
and always reached out

to touch the man of sorrows
who was acquainted with our infirmity.
(Cel 2, LI-LII)

All Through the Day

Believe me:
Whatever you do
to the least of my brothers and sisters,
you do to me.

(Mt 25:40)

My Day Is Ending

Our Father who art in heaven,
if I would see the face of your Son,
I need only look around.
You are everywhere.
Whenever I see the poor,
whenever I see the sick and homeless
or those without enough clothing
to cover them from the weather,
you are there
and they have a right to expect from me
your compassion.
Let me reach out to them
as you daily reach out to me.
And now as the day ends and sleep approaches,

open my heart to those in need.

For all your children
but especially for the poor and the homeless I pray:
Lord bless and keep all of us,
make your face to shine upon us
and be gracious to us.
Look kindly, Lord, upon us,
grant us a quiet night and lasting peace.

Day Twenty-Three

My Day Begins

Here is how Francis prayed.
He strove constantly
to stay consciously in the presence of God,
to break down the walls between heaven and earth.
With his whole soul he thirsted after Christ
and committed not just his soul
but his whole body to him as well.

To do this he prayed always.

When the needs of others prevailed,
he would never "end" his prayer,
but rather briefly interrupt it
and return to the innermost part of his being
at the first opportunity.
Living in the presence of God, as he did,
the world lost its savor for him.

He would seek out hidden places
where not only his soul but also his body
could be comfortable when his Lord visited him.
He was determined not to make a show of grace.
He would hide his face from others
and, if he could not hide,
he would retreat to the temple of his soul.
Never in the presence of others

would he betray his spiritual gifts
by outward displays of emotion.
But alone, out of the sight of others
it was a different matter.
He surrendered his whole self
to the presence of God
unembarrassed by tears, by shouts,
by words spoken aloud to the Lord.
He would petition his father,
talk with his friend,
and be joyful with his spouse.

He sought not to pray but to become a prayer.
(2 Cel 2 LXI)

All Through the Day

Rejoice always,
pray constantly,
give thanks in all things.

(1 Thess 16-17)

My Day Is Ending

Our Father who art in heaven,
you are everywhere on earth.
Your kingdom has no walls,
your presence no boundaries.
You are always with me,
even when I am least aware of you.
You are my father,
you are my friend,
you are my spouse.
You are my constant companion.
Let me pray always,
especially now
as the day ends and sleep approaches.

Keep open my eyes to your presence,
my ears to your voice.
May I and all your children always be aware of you.
Bless and keep all of us.
Make your face to shine upon us
and be gracious to us.
Look kindly, Lord, upon us,
grant us a quiet night and lasting peace,
conscious of your presence to the end.

Day Twenty-Four

◆◆◆◆◆

My Day Begins

For Francis prayer was nourishment
and the time of prayer should be a time
of peace and tranquillity.
To be distracted at prayer
was for him deeply upsetting,
a fault that he felt should be confessed immediately.
Anything, in fact, that took away from his concentration
he removed from his sight.
One day, for example, he found himself turning

to look at a small vase he had made.
When prayer was done he got rid of the vase.
" We should be ashamed," he said,
"to be caught up in worthless flights of imagination
when we are speaking with our sovereign Lord."

When he returned from prayer,
Francis would almost seem to be another person,
but he made every effort to fit in with others.
It was almost as though he was afraid
that if he let his special graces show,
he might lose them.
He would tell close friends
that when it came time to return to be with the others,
he would turn to God:
"Take these great consolations

that you have given me in this life
and keep them for me until the next.
"For," he said, "no matter how great our gifts from God,
we must let others see how poor we still are.
For the small reward of impressing others,
we must not lose the gift itself."
When others asked him to pray for them,
he treated it as an obligation
to be fulfilled as soon as possible.
Our spiritual love for each other, our charity,
should prompt us to make little gifts to each other.
To help others and to be helped by them
along our spiritual journey,
to commend and to be commended
before the face of Christ,
is the ultimate proof of our love.
(2 Cel 2 LXII-LXVII)

All Through the Day

To truly fulfill the law
according to the scripture,
you must love your neighbor as yourself.

(Jas 2:8)

My Day Is Ending

Our Father who art in heaven,
the proof of our love for you is always the same:
that we love one another as you have loved us,
that we love each other
as we love ourselves,
that along the way of our spiritual journey,
we are generous in helping others
and humble enough to accept their help.
Even as we want nothing to distract us from prayer,
let nothing turn us aside from love of neighbor.
Now as the day ends and sleep approaches,
remind me how poor I still am,
but out of my poverty

let me always be generous in love
to your children as you have been generous to me.

Bless and keep all of us.
Make your face to shine upon us
and be gracious to us.
Look kindly upon us,
grant us a quiet night, lasting peace,
and generosity of heart.

Day Twenty-Five

◆◆◆◆◆

My Day Begins

Francis had no formal education.
What he had was the gift of divine wisdom
that gave him a profound insight into the scriptures.
He was a spiritual genius
who entered easily into the profound mysteries of faith.
The knowledge of scholars is external.
The spiritual knowledge of Francis
allowed him to enter into the mystery itself.

He needed to read a scriptural passage only once
and it would be engraved indelibly on his heart.
His memory was his library.
He heard nothing in vain
and would meditate on the spiritual truths he heard
with deep and constant devotion.
He taught that this was the way to spiritual knowledge,
not reading your way through thousands of pages.

A true philosopher, he taught,
was someone who put nothing
before his search after eternal life.
But he also taught his companions
that anyone who read the scriptures
with humility and without presumption

would come to know not only himself but God also.
Once a great doctor of theology came to Francis
to pose a difficult question.
At first Francis hesitated in the face of his visitor's scholarship
but then replied from his knowledge of scripture.
The learned man was deeply moved.
He returned to his companions to say:
"The theology of this man arises
from his purity of life and his contemplation.
It is like a soaring eagle.
Compared to his, our learning is earthbound."
(2 Cel 2, LXVIII-LXIX)

All Through the Day

I am the light of the world;
if you follow me
you will not walk in darkness,
but in the light of life.

(Jn 8:12)

My Day Is Ending

Our Father who art in heaven,
anchor and enrich my faith
with the gift of wisdom.
Let me read and meditate on your scriptures
with humility and without presumption,
but with deeper understanding.
Let me enter more easily into the mysteries of faith.
Let me be wise with your wisdom,
putting nothing before my search for eternal life.
Now as the day ends and sleep approaches,
let me be patient as you are
with my ignorance and shallowness,
my trust in earthly learning.

Bless all your children with divine wisdom
and keep us in your care.

Make your face to shine upon us
and be gracious to us.
Look kindly upon us,
grant us a quiet night
and lasting peace.

Day Twenty-Six

◆◆◆◆◆

My Day Begins

St. Francis believed firmly
that the best protection against temptation
was spiritual joy.
"The devil is delighted
when he can steal such joy from a soul
and goes about trying always to sow discord and doubt
because when your soul is joyful he is powerless.
The devil cannot enter a soul that is filled with joy,
but when we are downcast, sad, and discouraged

we are easily overcome by what troubles us
or we turn to other things."

Francis, therefore, worked constantly
to keep himself in good spirits,
the joy of the Spirit in his soul.
He avoided every trace of discouragement or depression,
turning quickly to prayer
the moment it appeared.
"The moment you are disturbed
in mind or soul in any way,
pray immediately
that you might recall and stay
in the presence of God
until your spiritual joy is restored."
Francis had a special affection for the joyful.

So important to him for a true spiritual life
was joy of spirit
that he made it part of his rule for his brothers and sisters.

"Do not go about with a gloomy countenance
or a hypocritical sadness.
Rather let the world see your joy in the Spirit.
Show everyone the fruits of the Spirit,
good cheer,
and generosity."
(2 Cel 2, XCI)

All Through the Day

In your presence
my heart is glad
and my soul full of joy.

(Ps 16: 9)

My Day Is Ending

Our Father who art in heaven,
let there be joy in my heart
and on my face.
Let nothing steal it from my soul.
Remind me always
and let the world know from my example
that true joy and good cheer,
not a woeful countenance
are the gifts you give
to those who live in your presence.
Now as the day ends and sleep approaches,
replace any discouragements of this day
with your joyful presence.

Bless and keep all your children in good cheer.
Let us not be downcast as darkness descends,
but catch us up in your joy.
Make your face to shine upon us
and be gracious to us.
Look kindly upon us,
grant us a quiet night
and lasting, joyful peace.

Day Twenty-Seven

My Day Begins

As anxious as Francis was to leave this world
which he saw as a place of temporary exile,
he saw in it not just a place of potential danger
but a shining image of its Creator's goodness.

He saw the Artist in the art.
He saw the Maker in all that he made.
He rejoiced in the works of the Lord
and looked through them
to see the source of their being and their life.

In everything beautiful
he saw Beauty itself.
To him all things were good
because they had been created by goodness itself.
In all things he recognized and followed
the footsteps of their Creator—his beloved.
From all things he made a ladder
on which to approach the King of Kings.
In all things he found God and begged them
to join him in praise of their Creator.

In candles and lamps
he found a symbol of the Eternal Light
and so wished that they might never be extinguished.
He walked gently on the earth
because of him who was called the Rock.

He instructed his companions
never to cut down a whole tree
so that it might bloom again.
And in the vegetable garden
he insisted that a small patch be set aside
for beautiful, sweet flowers
so that all who looked upon it
would be reminded of their sweet source.
In the beauty of creation
he saw the beauty
of the father of all things.
(2 Cel 2 CXXIV)

All Through the Day

All things were created
through and for him
and in him all things
are held together.

(Col 1:16)

My Day Is Ending

Our Father who art in heaven,
in all that you have made,
I see your beauty.
The world that I often see as my enemy
is a mirror of your love,
a shining image of your goodness and generosity.
You are the artist,
we are your art, the work of your hands.
Let me rejoice in this great truth.
Looking at your world,
let me see you its maker.
In the beauty of created things
let me recognize the beauty of the Creator,

the presence of the maker of us all.
Now as the day ends and sleep approaches,
Bless and keep all that you have created.
Make your face to shine upon your creation
and be gracious to it
and to us.

Look kindly, Father, upon us, your children,
grant us a quiet night and lasting peace.

Day Twenty-Eight

◆◆◆◆◆

My Day Begins

It should not surprise us
that Francis, who thought of himself
as a brother to all of creation,
loved even more deeply
those who are made in the image of God.

Nothing was more important to him
than the salvation of souls.
In this he, in a very special way,
imitated Christ who had died on the cross for souls.

For the salvation of souls
he struggled at prayer,
preached tirelessly, and
unendingly set an example.
A friend of Christ
loves the souls that Christ loves.
In fear and in love he concerned himself
with those who followed him,
lest having left the world behind,
they should also lose heaven.
Forgetful of himself,
his first concern was always
for the salvation of his companions.

That others might live, he lived a hard life
knowing that actions are more believable

and instructive than words.
Actions speak more sweetly,
persuade more easily,
show others the way with more certitude.
Though we speak
with the tongues of men and angels,
but do not show charity,
it profits us little
and others not at all.
(2 Cel 2, CXXXI)

All Through the Day

We live in faith, hope, and love,
these three;
but the greatest of these is love.

(1 Cor 13:13)

My Day Is Ending

Our Father who art in heaven,
it does little good
to pray with the words you have taught us,
if we do not love and sacrifice
for those whom you love
and for whom your Son sacrificed everything.
"A friend of Christ
loves the souls that Christ loves."
It profits us little, and others not at all
unless our lives speak
more loudly than our words.
Now as the day ends
and sleep approaches,
remind me that without love,

faith and hope are empty,
as are these words I pray.

Bless and keep all your children
especially those most in need of your love.
Make your face to shine upon us all
and be gracious to us.
Look kindly upon us,
grant us a quiet night and lasting peace.

Day Twenty-Nine

My Day Begins

If a single virtue characterized the life of Francis,
it was the guardian of all other virtues,
humility.
To others he might seem a saint.
In his own eyes he was still a sinner.
This conviction was
the foundation of his spiritual growth.
The Son of God,
he often reminded his companions and sisters,

forsook the side of his Father
to share in our humanity
in order to teach us humility
by word and example.
He believed to imitate Christ
he must not only think humbly of himself
but ensure that others shared this view.
There are, he knew,
those who prove themselves
in their neighbor's eyes,
but God knows their hearts.

"For what is exalted among men
is an abomination before God."

(1 Cor 16:15)

PEACE OF HEART

Whatever you are in the sight of God,
that is who you are.
To be puffed up by the praise of others is foolish.
It is silly to expect praise or take pride
in what even sinners can do.
A sinner can fast, pray, weep, and do penance.
The only thing a sinner can't do
is to remain faithful to God.
Don't expect or accept praise that is due only to God.
Rather serve God faithfully
and direct to him
the praise that might come your way
and gratitude for his gifts.

All Through the Day

You are Christ's,
and Christ is God's.

(1 Cor. 3:22-23)

My Day Is Ending

Our Father who art in heaven,
I am who I am,
not in the eyes of the world
which is so easy to please and displease,
but in your eyes.
Your Son left your side to share in our humanity
in order to teach us humility.
It is a hard lesson to learn, but until I do
I will always be in danger of trying to be
someone other than who I am in your eyes.
However I appear to the world,
I am still a sinner.
Now as the day ends and sleep approaches,

consider the poverty of my soul
and uproot my pride.

Bless and keep all your children
in true humility.
Make your face to shine upon us
and be gracious to us.
Look kindly upon us,
grant us a quiet night and lasting peace.

Day Thirty

◆◆◆◆◆

My Day Begins

Francis sought Christ with a burning passion
that completely absorbed him.
Just the mention of the "love of God" was enough
to rekindle the fire in his soul.
To offer the love of God to someone
in exchange for alms seemed to him
to be a gesture worthy of the most wealthy.
To think money more important than love
was for him the height of foolishness.

Only love can win the kingdom of heaven.

The image of the crucified Christ
was burned into his heart
and he desired more than anything else,
by the power of love,
to become like Christ.
Christ was always in his sight.
And his love for Christ was exceeded
only by the love Christ had for him.

◆◆◆◆◆

Pray for us therefore, St. Francis,
as surrounded by a thousand dangers,

we try to follow your example.
Pray for us that our Father in heaven
will grant us the strength
we will need,
that our motives will be pure,
that our lives will be filled with joy.

Pray
that a spirit of compassion and prayer
will be granted to us.

May we imitate you
in your humility,
in your poverty,
and in the great love
with which you always loved Christ crucified,

and all his creatures,
great and small.

With you
we ask this in the name
of that same Christ
who with the Father
and the Holy Spirit
lives and reigns
world without end.
Amen.

(From the Prayer of Francis' Companions)

All Through the Day

Grant me a spirit
of humility and compassion,
and in my heart
a peace that will last.

My Day Is Ending

Our Father who art in heaven,
only love can win your kingdom.
Burn into my heart
a desire to become like your Son.
I will be surrounded by a thousand dangers
as I try to become like him.
Grant me the strength I will need
to keep my motives pure
and my life filled with joy.
Give me the compassion I will need
to love others as you love me,
and a spirit of prayer
that never forgets your presence.
Now as this day ends and sleep approaches

nourish in my soul
all that I have learned from Francis.

Bless me and all his brothers and sisters
especially the poor.
Make your face to shine upon us,
and be gracious to us.
Look kindly upon us,
grant us a quiet night and lasting peace.

One Final Word

This book was created to be nothing more than a gateway—a gateway to the spiritual wisdom of a specific teacher, and a gateway opening on your own spiritual path.

You may decide that Francis of Assisi is someone whose experience of God is one that you wish to follow more closely and deeply. In that case you should get a copy of the entire text of *The Little Flowers* or a good biography of the saint, or one of dozens of other books about his teachings. Pray it as you have prayed this journey.

You may decide that his experience has not helped you. There are many other teachers. Somewhere there is the right teacher for your own, very special, absolutely unique journey of the spirit. You *will* find your teacher, you *will* discover your path.

We would not be searching, as St. Augustine reminds us, if we had not already found.

One more thing should be said.

Spirituality is not meant to be self-absorption, a cocoonish relationship of God and me. In the long run, if it is to have meaning, if it is to grow and not wither, it must be a wellspring of compassionate living. It must reach out to others as God has reached out to us.

True spirituality breaks down the walls of our souls and lets in not just heaven, but the whole world.

A powerful reminder of this basic spiritual truth is captured in the Prayer for Peace that is attributed (without real evidence) to St. Francis. Here, for this moment and purpose, its authorship is not important. Its message is what matters. It reminds us that true spirituality reaches out to all the children of God, that it does not end in our own consolation but in that all embracing love for others that we call compassion.

Peace is for peacemakers.

A Prayer for Peace.

Lord, make me an instrument of your peace.
Where there is hatred, let me sow love;
where there is injury, pardon;
where there is doubt, faith;
where there is despair, hope;
where there is darkness, light;
and where there is sadness, joy.
O Divine Master, grant that I may not so much seek
to be consoled as to console,
to be understood as to understand,
to be loved as to love.

For it is giving that we receive,

it is in pardoning that we are pardoned,

and it is in dying that we are born to eternal life.

Amen.

So be it.